Old LISBURN

by
John Hanna

Around the turn of the twentieth century the Royal Irish Fusiliers chose a market day to parade through Lisburn to foster support for the Boer War. In this view, taken from George Duncan's shop in Market Square, the chimney of Stewart's thread mill, built in 1888, can be seen in the right background. This mill was demolished in the early 1980s. On the skyline to the left is the Catholic chapel, built in 1900; its spire was added in 1939. Looking towards Bow Street, on the left-hand corner stands the fine building which housed Hugh Kirkwood's hardware and ironmongery warehouse. This eighteenth century building was later demolished.

Text © John Hanna, 2002
First published in the United Kingdom, 2002,
by Stenlake Publishing,
Telephone / Fax: 01290 551122

ISBN 1 84033 227 1

FURTHER READING

The books listed below were used by the author during his research. None of them are available from Stenlake Publishing. Those interested in finding out more are advised to contact their local bookshop or reference library.
May Blair, *Once upon the Lagan*, 1981.
E.R.R. Green, *The Lagan Valley 1800–1850*, 1949.
Mavis Heaney, *Lisburn Life in the County Down*, 1996.
Brian Mackey, *Lisburn – The Town and its People*, 2000.
Neville H. Newhouse, *A History of Friends' School*, 1974.
The Linen Thread Company, *The Faithful Fibre*.

ACKNOWLEDGEMENTS

The publishers wish to thank Des Quail for providing the photographs which appear in this book.

The author wishes to thank the following for their assistance: Pat Browne, Librarian of Friends' School, George Scott of Hillhall Presbyterian Church, Kenneth Clarke, and Cecil Walker of Lisburn Cricket Club.

The Assembly Buildings, seen here from the top of Bridge Street, began as a market house in 1707 and was the only building to escape the great fire of that year. When the building was expanded in the 1880s wings were added to the market house and its original arches may be seen inside the expanded structure. The Assembly Room was added later as a second floor and was used for assemblies, balls and dinners. The room had seven large windows, three chandeliers, two fireplaces and a dais for musicians. Guests entered through a fine wooden door which is all that remains of the original room after it was remodelled in 1985. The clock tower was added by the second Marquis of Hertford in the early 1800s.

INTRODUCTION

In March 2002, Her Majesty the Queen, Queen Elizabeth II, granted City status to Lisburn, but to begin to look at the history of the town one has to go back to the reign of Queen Elizabeth I. During her reign many Irish chieftains were rebelling against English rule in Ireland and among these was the chief of Killultagh whose stronghold was the tiny village of Lis-na-garvoch. Queen Elizabeth sent over armies to quell this last rising of Gaelic Ireland and after their victory many of her soldiers were rewarded with local lands.

Killultagh passed into the hands of Sir Fulke Conway and he invited English and Welsh tenants to settle in the village of Lisnagarvey. He built Conway Castle and surrounded it with fifty-three tenements which constituted the settlement. Sir Fulke left no children and after his death his estate was inherited by his elder brother, Sir Edward, later the first Viscount Conway. He had close ties with King Charles I and obtained a royal charter which granted market rights in 1628. Since that time weekly markets have been held in Lisburn on Tuesdays. In 1631 the second Viscount appointed George Rawdon as his agent in Ireland and for over half a century this man was responsible for the steady development of the town.

By the time of the great rebellion in 1641, Bridge Street, Castle Street and the Market Square had been built, forming the basic town plan of what was to become modern Lisburn. During the rebellion the town remained loyal to England and George Rawdon led its defence, during which many rebels were slaughtered. The town, however, which was mostly comprised of wooden buildings, was destroyed by fire and it was after this that its name began to change to Lisburn.

The town recovered quickly and attracted many new settlers from Britain, mainly from the north of England. Between 1660, the time of the Restoration of King Charles II, and the early part of the eighteenth century, Lisburn experienced phenomenal expansion. In 1662 its status was enhanced by a royal charter which constituted its simple church as a cathedral and the town as a parliamentary borough, enabling the election of two members to the Irish Parliament. Rawdon continued to ensure careful planning and regulation in the growth of the town and by the time the Duke of Schomberg, the Williamite commander, chose the town as his campaign headquarters in 1689, Lisburn was described as 'one of the prettiest inland towns in Ireland'.

In 1707 another great fire destroyed most of Lisburn in just half an hour one Sunday morning. Even the castle was burnt to the ground and was never rebuilt. But once again the town managed to recover quickly and by 1725 the population had grown to 3,700, making it the eighth largest town in Ireland. While the town's street plan was basically unaltered, many new houses, some of them four storeys high, were built. Castle Street became the elite area with doctors, magistrates and linen manufacturers residing there alongside the residence of the Marquis of Hertford to whom the territory had by this time reverted. Living conditions were not so comfortable, however, for those who were crowded into the entries and alleyways along Bridge Street.

During the eighteenth century Lisburn continued to be a busy market town and the Linen Hall was built to cater for the town's thriving brown linen market. This prosperity was due largely to Louis XIV of France persecuting French Protestants, or Huguenots, in 1685. Many of them fled their country and settled throughout the Lagan Valley and one of them, Louis Crommelin, set up a model manufactory to promote the establishment of fine weaving. Another factor in this industrial growth was the abolition of a tax which had previously been applied to Irish linen exported to England. Then, in 1765, the Lagan Navigation Canal was opened from Belfast to Lisburn, allowing coal to be brought cheaply to the town. Further large-scale production followed. William Coulson established his first linen looms in 1764 and in 1784 a Scot, John Barbour, began spinning linen thread. By 1787 Lisburn had a weekly linen market that was the second largest in Ulster after Lurgan. In 1789 another Scot, James Wallace, bought the first steam engine to be seen in Ireland and installed it in his cotton spinning mill just off of Castle Street. In addition to the impact of the Industrial Revolution, Lisburn also benefited from the arrival of the railway from Belfast in 1839. A measure of the town's success was the fact that while throughout the nineteenth century the Hertford family were effectively absentee landlords, the fourth marquis was receiving £55,000 a year net rental from his estate!

Towards the end of the century a new owner with a different outlook inherited the estate. Sir Richard Wallace arrived in 1873 and was responsible for many new buildings, either by building them himself or by granting sites for churches, halls and parks all over the town. At this time many new mill houses were also being built for those arriving to find employment in the expanding mills. In 1898 the Local Government Act enabled the establishment of the Lisburn Urban District Council and, despite periods of anxiety in the twentieth century and the loss of some fine buildings due to redevelopment over the years, Lisburn has continued its economic growth ever since.

This wonderful façade was added to the building of George Duncan and Sons' drapery warehouse (built in the 1880s) in the centre of Market Square in the early part of the twentieth century. The plaque above the centre window was rescued from the first fire in 1707 and is now inside the museum. To the right of the picture the lamp-post is a 'Jubilee Lamp', now gone, which had been erected to commemorate the Diamond Jubilee of Queen Victoria in 1897. Just behind it is one of the two fountains Sir Richard Wallace presented to he town. This is still in place. At the time this photograph was taken the entrance to the cathedral in the background was very narrow, but the Temperance Hotel, which belonged to R. Fitzsimons and Son, was later demolished to give better access.

Market Square has been the site of the weekly general market since market rights were granted to Edward, Viscount Conway and Killultagh, by King Charles I in 1628. Ownership of the market site was transferred to the Town Commissioners in 1849 and then to Lisburn Urban Council in 1898. The market moved to the Smithfield area in the 1930s and with the building of the new town square in 2001 has once again relocated to a smaller site near Smithfield. In this photograph, taken some time after 1922, H.P. sauce appears to be in ample supply at the nearest stall and it is clear that buyers had a wide range of products to choose from, including chinaware, glassware, drapery and hardware. Many of the buildings to the right of Market Square have survived.

In 1949 a fire destroyed the upper floors of the building in the centre of the square, but these were rebuilt and named the Ulster Buildings on reopening. Those trading there included Tweedy Acheson and Co., outfitters, and the Corner Café. The buildings were demolished in 1992 to make way for the Irish Linen Centre and Museum. In the centre of the square is the statue of Brigadier General John Nicholson, a native of Lisburn. Born in December 1822, he was killed leading an assault on Delhi during the Indian Mutiny in 1857. Designed by F.W. Pomeroy, the statue was a gift to the town from Henry Musgrave, a Lisburn-born benefactor of Belfast who died a few weeks before it was unveiled in 1922. The buildings to the left remain as they are except for the premises of the Belfast Banking Co. Ltd which has been replaced by a more recent building. In the early 1950s, the period when this photograph was taken, Market Square and Bow Street were one of the first one-way road systems in Ulster. The area is now a pedestrian zone.

The Harvey and Maxwell families were related to one another and at one time they operated an off-licence and grocer's shop. While it has a late Victorian façade, this building dates from the eighteenth century and still exists in Market Square although it is now a shop. This photograph shows the shop in 1910.

In this view of Castle Street, looking towards Market Square, a bus belonging to the Ulster Motor Service Company is just passing Castle Gardens in which stands the war memorial. The two tall buildings just past the trees of the park were built in the 1780s and still stand today. The first was at one time a Masonic hall, while the one next door was the cathedral rectory. The railings of Castle House are on the right of the photograph. Castle House became the Municipal Technical Institute in 1914. Later renamed the Lisburn Institute, the buildings on the right with the steps were demolished in order to extend it.

8

In 1905, when this photograph was taken, Castle Street was the most fashionable street in Lisburn, being home to the wealthier citizens. The house at the end of the row, with the two storey Victorian porch, was the birthplace of John Doherty Barbour, the eldest son of the linen thread manufacturer, William Barbour. These fine houses were the ones, also pictured on the previous page, which were demolished to make way for the extension to the Lisburn Institute. Just past the park on the right stood the convent of Sacred Heart of Mary, established by French nuns in 1870. It closed one hundred years later and tragically was demolished. It is now a car park.

This is the junction of Bridge Street and Market Square East, looking down to where the bridge crossed the River Lagan. As can be seen, the street at one time contained a wide variety of shops. The first shop on the left is that of Robert Dickey, the flesher. Next door were the premises of Mrs. C. Pelan, a wine and spirit merchant, which later became the Bridge Bar and is now the Old Book Shop. Next to her were two grocers, Will Cruickshank and Samuel Green. On the other side of the road was Dornan Brothers, the butchers, and next to them were the premises of W. Ritchie and Co. who also ran the Paragon Tea House on the first floor.

Bridge Street is one of the oldest streets in Lisburn, leading from where the first bridges crossed the River Lagan to the centre of the town. In this view of the street's lower end, on the right, by the lamp-post, are the premises of J. Jefferson, a confectioner, while next door is the shop of William Wright, a bird specialist. The lowest shop with the awning is that of J. McCoubrey, a baker and grocer. On the left-hand side is the Old Castle Bar owned by Abraham Keery. This building is now derelict after it was sold about four years ago in order that its licence could be used for a new bar close by. Bridge Street is at the heart of the Lisburn Historical Development Strategy, a scheme which aims to protect this historical part of town.

These houses on Low Road were typical mill workers' houses for those employed in the nearby Island Spinning Mill. The houses on the left, beyond the railings, are known as Eagle Terrace. The William Foote Memorial School is on the near left, behind the railings, and was connected to Seymour Street Methodist Church. Foote was a grocer in the town and left money for the building of the school after his death. It stood from 1906 to 1999 when it was demolished and replaced with a new church building. Apart from this, the scene has changed very little, although this part of Low Road is now called Wesley Street.

Ballynahinch Road, looking towards Young Street and the town centre. All of these houses are still standing, but the well-tended gardens with their monkey puzzle trees and shrubs have gone. This road was at one time the main road from Lisburn to Ballynahinch, but the building of the M1 motorway in 1963 blocked it just behind the point where this photograph was taken.

An early picture of Bow Street, taken at a time when there was still one building with a thatched roof (in the middle of the row on the left). Among the row on the right was the emigration office for William Barbour where those wishing to travel to Paterson, New Jersey, to work in the Barbour factory there could arrange to do so. Another office on this street was the Lisburn Servants' Registry where domestic employment could be obtained. In 1819 Bow Street was described as one of the busiest streets in Lisburn and at that time, in addition to eleven public houses, the street contained the premises of the main tradesmen such as the carpenters and shoemakers. For example, a boot and shoe merchant, David Kilpatrick, was based at No. 65.

14

Bow Street in the 1930s, viewed from the junction with Antrim Street and looking towards Market Square. Many of these buildings were destroyed in bomb attacks on the town in 1972. Up to that time the lion still hung above the entrance to the Golden Lion Tea House on the right. On the left, Anderson's was owned by John E. Anderson who was a newsagent for the *Belfast News-Letter* and the *Belfast Weekly News*. The tall building on the left with the ornate upper façade replaced the thatched building shown on the previous page and was at one time the offices of the *Lisburn Herald* newspaper.

William Croskery of 61 Bow Street was a grocer who specialised in tea. He began trading in the latter part of the nineteenth century and by 1930 the shop had changed hands. Above these premises Croskery ran the Golden Lion Tea House, outside of which hung the golden lion.

This photograph and the one on the next page were taken by Lisburn photographer John Lannigan and show the destruction of property in the town which followed the murder of District Inspector Swanzy of the Royal Irish Constabulary in August 1920. He was shot dead in front of the Northern Bank in Railway Street and most of the property subsequently destroyed belonged to members of the Roman Catholic community (it was a revenge killing ordered by Michael Collins). Here in Bow Street the main targets were the public houses, including those of Thomas Browne, whiskey bonder and wine importer, and Todd Brothers, grocers and spirit merchants. These premises were looted before being burnt and the subsequent drunkenness led to even more trouble.

The scene of destruction on the other side of Bow Street where Redmond Jefferson's saw mill was possibly an accidental casualty of the sectarian burning of buildings as he was not Catholic.

Seymour Street is another example in the town today where attractive buildings have been demolished in the name of progress. The first six buildings on the left have been replaced by the headquarters of the Fire Authority for Northern Ireland. Fortunately, the older buildings further down remain. Just past the small cottage was a nurses' home, presented to the County Antrim Infirmary by the people of Lisburn as a memorial of both the Golden and Diamond jubilees of Queen Victoria (these occurred in 1887 and 1897 respectively). The Infirmary was the three storey building down from it next door. The hospital moved to this site in the early 1800s and in 1882 a Dr George St George was appointed as its chief. He improved the hospital greatly with the help of funds from the Barbour family. This building is now restored as dwellings. The large buildings making up the row on the near right of the picture have been replaced with motor showrooms.

In the centre background of this 1934 photograph is Seymour Street Methodist Church, at the street's junction with the Belfast and Hilden roads. John Wesley first preached to the people of Lisburn in the Market House in 1758. After establishing a church in Market Street, the Methodist congregation were given this site 'free of rent for ever' by Sir Richard Wallace. Built in 1875 at a cost of £4,000, the church is of Venetian Gothic style. The bus in the foreground belonged to the Belfast Omnibus Company. It has just passed the motor showroom of Stevenson Brothers, the site of which is now derelict.

Railway Street was formerly known as Jackson's Lane. The bridge across the railway line can be seen beside the station at the bottom of the street. The Castle Buildings on the corner with Castle Street were designed by local architect William Sands in 1890 and were for many years the premises of Alexander Boyd and Co. Ltd, encompassing a pharmacy, grocery store and coal supplier. The grocery closed in 1973, but the pharmacy remained open until 1988. On the opposite corner is the Lisburn branch of the Northern Bank. This building has since been modified and is now the premises of Shannon's jewellers.

William Henry Mills was the architect of the Great Northern Railway's station in Lisburn. A single storey yellow brick building, it was erected around 1890 and replaced the original station which had been built in 1839. That year the railway journey from Belfast to Lisburn was the first in Ulster, being established just a decade after the introduction of passenger traffic in Britain. Waiting for passengers was a jaunting car, one of many at that time which provided local transport in Lisburn.

A busy scene at Lisburn Station in 1907 as a North British railmotor arrives from Belfast. The Great Northern Railway introduced these trains on local lines in response to the electrification of trams in Belfast in 1905 (an improvement which made 1,000 horses redundant). The railmotor was supposed to have a fast turnaround, enabling people working in Belfast to return home to Lisburn for lunch! The journey took twenty-six minutes when stopping at all stations en route, including three new halts at Finaghy, Derriaghy and Hilden which were opened for the service.

Bachelor's Walk was a smart residential part of the town with neatly maintained pathways and gardens. Many of the buildings on the right still exist, but nearly all have commercial properties or offices in the lower floors. In between the rear of these houses and the railway line was a factory owned by Miller and Stevenson and this linen company owned many of these houses. The buildings at the end of the street, in the centre background, were in Antrim Road and have been demolished.

BATCHELORS' WALK, COURT HOUSE AND INSTITUTE, LISBURN.

All the houses on the left of Bachelor's Walk, from the entrance to the saw mills and coal yard (on the near left) to the top of the street, are still in place. Probably the greatest act of civic vandalism to have taken place in Lisburn was the demolition in 1971 of Sir Richard Wallace's courthouse at the far end of the street. It had been built in 1901. On the corner opposite it was the Temperance Institute, built in 1890 on a site given, again by Sir Richard Wallace, to the Lisburn Temperance Union (established in 1887). Its function was to provide constructive alternatives to alcohol use. Since the 1980s it has been the Bridge Community Centre.

The Lisburn Co-operative was established in 1882 and its premises were at 27 Castle Street, next to the town hall. In 1905 the society amalgamated with the Working Men's Club, which was also next door, and was able to provide recreational facilities such as billiard tables, a shooting range, and library. A brass band was also formed. The society employed quite a large number of men and women and their first president was Harold Barbour. It was later taken over by the Belfast Co-operative Society.

John Hancock was a wealthy Quaker linen merchant and in 1764 he left £1,000 for the purchase of land in or around Lisburn for the building of a school. His will stipulated that the school was 'for the education of the youth of the people called Quakers, the master thereof to be a sober and reputable person, and one of said people'. Twenty acres for the school were purchased at Prospect Hill from the Earl of Hertford and, named the Ulster Provincial School, it was established in 1774. In 1794 it became the responsibility of the Ulster Quaker Meeting. The school later changed its name to Friends' School and has become one of the leading grammar schools in Northern Ireland. These buildings still form a major part of the school and in the 1920s, when this photograph was taken, the wing to the left was for the boys and the one to the right was for the girls.

By 1900 Friends' School was enrolling non-Quaker children as well. Many of the pupils were boarders and their education was based on a varied curriculum. As early as 1848 (when the school was still called the Ulster Provincial School) a workshop with a lathe was built for the boys. The workroom cost £15 14s. 10d. to build and by 1889 it was recorded that 'the carpentry and wood-carving done by the boys were noted with much interest, and the teaching of them commended'. This photograph of the boys' workshop was taken around 1926. By 1929 the workshop had gone and the boys went to the Technical School in the town to get classes in woodwork.

The Snail Hunters

Boys of Friends' School engaged as 'snail hunters' along the towpath of the Lagan Navigation Canal. From its foundation, the staff of the school encouraged a great interest in natural history and outings such as this were common for both the boys and the girls.

In this view taken from Magheralave Road, the entrance gates to the twenty-five acre Wallace Park are on the left. The junction with North Circular Road is on the right. The spire of the cathedral and the cupola of the Assembly Buildings are just a short walk over the railway line by the Boyne Bridge to the centre of the town. The bridge replaced an earlier level crossing. Originally known as The People's Park, the park was given to the people of Lisburn by Sir Richard Wallace in 1884. He also paid for the building of the bandstand, entrance gates and lodges. The lodge at this gate has now been badly vandalised.

This lake is situated on an elevated site in a corner of Wallace Park close to Fort Hill Road and is surrounded by iron railings. On a map of 1854 it is shown as the town reservoir which accounts for its situation; some underground work recently unearthed the original wooden pipes! The building to the left was part of Friends' School, but has been replaced by new buildings. The house behind the trees remains. Unfortunately, the lake is no longer treated with the same care and attention as it was receiving at the time of this photograph.

While a cricket and tennis club was formed in Lisburn in 1854, these grass courts in Wallace Park were not actually in use until 1884. They were situated at the rear of the cricket pavilion. There was no netting around the courts, but it looks as though a ball boy was situated at each end to return balls to the server.

Castle Gardens & Wallace Monument, Lisburn.

Lisburn's other park, Castle Gardens, is situated on the site of the original castle, opposite the Lisburn Institute which at the time of this photograph was still Castle House. The gardens were given to the town council in 1901 by Lady Wallace's heir, Sir John Murray Scott. Lady Wallace's husband, Sir Richard, was very popular among his tenants in Lisburn and they subscribed to erect the Wallace Monument in his memory after his death in 1892. He was chiefly responsible for the development of the town in the late nineteenth century. The cannon in the gardens came from Sebastopol at the time of the Crimean War and was presented in 1858 by Admiral Meynell, a former MP for Lisburn. The chimney of the Island Spinning Mill can be seen in the background.

At one time this fountain in Castle Gardens was painted blue, with white painted egrets with red beaks, and red flowers. Today, it has lost its flowers and a little of its glamour. The spire of Christ Church Cathedral dominates this view. While its foundation stone was laid immediately after the fire in 1708, the spire was not added until 1807. It was built by David McBlain and the £2,000 cost was born by Francis Seymour Conway, the second Marquis of Hertford. The building to the left is part of the church buildings, while the tower to the right, which was probably on the parochial hall, has gone.

No. 13 lock on the Lagan Navigation Canal was known as Hogg's Lock after the family that operated the lock gates for many years. These included William Hogg from 1856 and later his wife Betty. Situated between Union Bridge and Moore's Bridge near where the Ravernet River joins the Lagan, the canal reached here in 1765. A sluice to control a mill race can be seen on the right of the lock and this is still visible today.

As well as linking Sloan Street with Bridge Street, the Union Bridge also links County Down with County Antrim. It was built in 1885 at a cost of £3,000 and replaced an earlier bridge which itself had replaced one built in the 1780s ninety yards downstream. On the right-hand bank is Sloan Street Presbyterian Church, situated at the corner with Young Street. Opened in 1900, it was designed by Henry Hobart of Dromore and cost £4,000 to build. On the riverside beside the church was the Co-operative Society coal yard and quay, on which stands a large cart. On the left bank is the original site of a corn mill and a canal barge is tied up at Piper's Quay. There is a new hostelry of that name on the site now. Piper's Hill led to the quay and took its name from the grisly incident in 1641 when a piper's head was severed by gun fire and rolled down the hill.

53302 (JV)

This view of the Lagan Navigation Canal was taken around 1913 and shows a horse-drawn lighter discharging its cargo, probably coal, at the Hilden linen yarn factory of Richardson, Sons and Owden (the lighterman had to rig up a set of sheerlegs to unload his cargo). In the mid-nineteenth century this company was one of the largest linen manufacturing firms in the world. To the left the canal leads to the locks at Lisburn. The spire of the cathedral is not far away, while the large chimney belongs to the Island Spinning Mill. The mill race can be seen close to the factory wall.

The Island Spinning Mill in Lisburn was situated on a three acre island between the Lagan Navigation Canal and the River Lagan. The canal is to the right, while to the left the River Lagan flows over a weir and a footbridge leads to the dye house and the thread department and also to an area close to Kilrush Cemetery. The original factory on the island was the Vitriol Works, producing vitriol for the bleaching of linen. This factory was purchased by Samuel Richardson and he built a steam-powered spinning mill in 1840. A powerloom weaving factory was added in 1871, but from 1882 until its closure in 1983, the Island Spinning Mill specialised in the production of linen thread. The mill was four stories high and in 1885 employed 1,100 people. The mill was demolished and in 1999 was replaced by the Island Civic Centre which was officially opened by Queen Elizabeth in November 2001. It now houses the offices of Lisburn District Council which moved from Hillsborough in 2000.

Barbour's mill on the Lagan Navigation Canal at Hilden, a few miles outside of Lisburn. The growth of William Barbour and Sons is a good example of the success of the Industrial Revolution in Ireland. In 1823 William Barbour bought a former bleach mill at Hilden and built a water-powered twisting mill. This became the largest linen thread mill in the world and by 1914 it employed around 2,000 people. The company built a model village for its workforce which consisted of 350 houses, two schools, a community hall, a children's playground and a village sports ground.

In 1784 John Barbour of Paisley, Scotland, established a linen thread works in Lisburn while his son, William, bought a derelict bleach green at Hilden and set up business. Later, he also transferred the thread works to Hilden and as early as 1817 was employing 122 workers. William died in 1875 and his eldest son, J. Doherty Barbour, succeeded him as managing director. In 1898 he formed the Linen Thread Company and this became a large international company. Another of William's sons, Thomas, founded a factory for the company in Paterson, New Jersey, in 1864. Among the Ulster company's varied products were nets which, as the other advert shows, could be made into snares and also fishing nets. These adverts appeared on postcards used by the company to communicate with customers. On the back of one of them is the message: 'Dear Sir, we beg to acknowledge, with thanks, your esteemed order. We will have it put in work and give it our best attention. Soliciting your further favours, yours truly, Wm. Barbour and Sons, Ltd.'

KILLULTAGH L.O.L. Nº 147

St Patrick's Roman Catholic Church on Chapel Hill which was formerly part of Bow Street. The first Chapel was built in 1786, but was demolished in 1900 and replaced with this fine building. A spire was added in 1939. A stone below the statue in the grounds states that 'the building fund was subscribed to by people of every religion in this country'. Next door is St Joseph's Hall which was demolished in 1998.

Killultagh Loyal Orange Lodge No. 147 was founded in the Ballinderry district in 1798 and this photograph from around 1909, taken outside Greenhall, the home of Dr Mockler near Ballinderry, shows the First Banner Unfurling ceremony. The members meet monthly on Saturday evenings 'on or before full moon' according to a tradition designed to assist the original members walking or cycling to and from meetings during darkness. Many of those pictured here have been identified. *Back row* (left to right): John Gawley, William James Allen, Edward Hanna, a man thought to be a Mr Ross, William McLernon, thought to be Mr Thompson, Ernie Kidd, Sandy Haddock, John Sefton, George Dickson, William Thompson, David Branagh, unknown, unknown; *middle row*: Tom Sefton, Adam Branagh, John Eddie McCullough, unknown, unknown, unknown, George McLernon, unknown, unknown, William Sefton; *front row*: unknown, unknown, unknown, John Thompson, thought to be James Beckett, William Henry Sefton, thought to be Mr Ross.

This is likely to be the flute band of the Lisburn Conservative Working Mens' Club, photographed in 1906. They had a band hall in Wallace Avenue where social evenings were held. While all the members of the band wore a uniform cap, the conductor, to the left, wore a bowler hat.

Another band, the Hillhall Unionist Flute Band, photographed in 1908 in front of Hillhall Presbyterian Church following a service of dedication. Some of the band members are known, but none of the four sitting on the ground can be named. In the front row the second from the left is T.A. McNeill, Albert Whitley is the bass drummer, T. McNeice is next to him, and on extreme right, standing, is W. Whitley. Extreme left in the second row is Joe Caughey. In the top row, from the left, are T. Ervine, E. Ferguson, H. Boyd, J. Shields and R. Spence. This photograph is another taken by John Lannigan, one of Lisburn's most prolific photographers. He was in business by the 1890s and operated a studio in Antrim Street before moving to Castle Street. He died in 1938.

This photograph of the Boys' Brigade was also taken by Lannigan shortly after the Rev. Gilmour Neill had formed the company in 1911. The windows and doors at the front of the Presbyterian Church in Hillhall, a village two miles outside Lisburn, have not changed since. The Rev. Gilmour Neill remained with the church until 1913. A later reverend, Archibald Duff, who was installed in 1925, created a fine tradition of Scouting in Hillhall. While none of the boys can be identified, a number of the officers can. In the second row, second from the left is Albert Whitley, the bass drummer from the photograph on the previous page, then James Armour and R. Waring. Next is the Rev. Gilmour Neill, while second from the right is J. Brown.

Cricket has been played in Lisburn since 1836, making the Lisburn Cricket Club the oldest in Northern Ireland. The club moved to The People's Park in Lisburn in 1854. In 1884, when Sir Richard Wallace presented the park to the town, the club fought hard to maintain the cricket ground and eventually four granite boundary stones were sunk to mark the perimeter, each marked 'R.W.' This photograph shows the Lisburn Cricket Club 2nd XI of 1926, winners that year of the Northern Cricket Union of Ireland 2nd Division Senior League. *Back row* (left to right): Joe Awty (Professional Coach), Tommy Martin, S.F. Megran, E. Browne, A.E. Hunter, C.O. Hobson, R.J. Barclay, Fullerton Keery; *middle row*: C.W. Smyth, J. Robinson, C.M. Allen (Capt.), H.N. Crook (Vice-Capt.), J.D.Crothers; *front row*: W.J. Waring, J. Jackson. Joe Awty was appointed Professional that year.

This photograph is of 'go-as-you-please' to Lurgan on 22 June 1907. The race was really a marathon, the distance described as 26 miles and several hundred yards. The journey had to be completed 'without extraneous assistance from vehicles'. With 461 competitors, the race began at the Markets in Belfast at 1 p.m. and these runners are turning out of Lisburn's Bow Street into Market Place. Contrary to expectations the first arrivals in Lurgan took just over three hours, the first three being F.W. Furlonger, Thomas McCullough, and a Corporal Sparks. One hundred and sixty runners finished before 6 p.m. and qualified for prizes. The promoter of the 1907 event was the *Ireland Saturday Night*, a Belfast sporting newspaper which tried unsuccessfully to revive the race in the 1950s. Premises in the background include those of Robert Taylor, a Singer sewing machine agent, P. McCourt, a coach manufacturer, William John Bailey, an auctioneer and house furnisher, John Dowey, a grocer, Jas. Coulter, a grocer and provisions merchant, and, on the corner of Antrim Street, Thomas Oliver, the wine and spirit merchant.

A highlight of the 1907 'go-as-you-please' was the motor car topped with posters for the Murray company's famous Front Bench cigarettes. Hundreds of packets of cigarettes were liberally distributed from the car and eagerly scrambled for by the spectators. After the car and the first of the competitors had passed through Lisburn one of the occupants of the car, dressed in a gold laced uniform and wearing on his hat the legend 'Front Bench easily wins', was dropped off to walk through the remaining towns and villages.

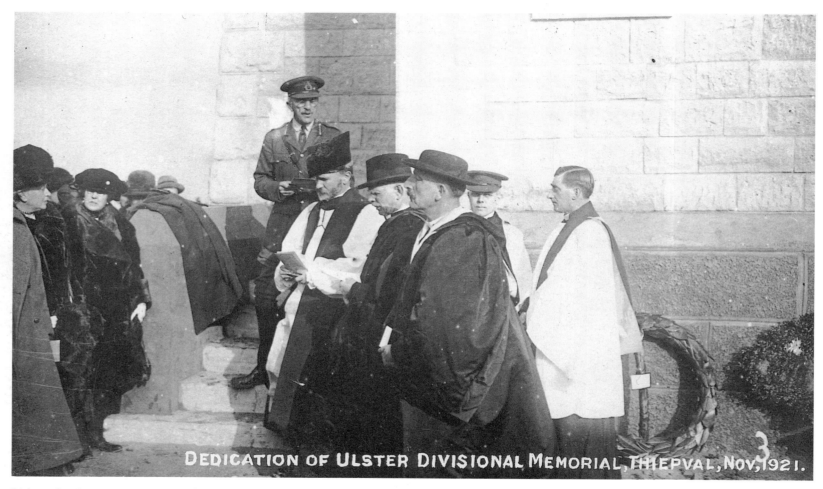

DEDICATION OF ULSTER DIVISIONAL MEMORIAL, THIEPVAL, NOV, 1921.

Lisburn has been a garrison town for a long time and the local barracks are called Theipval Barracks after the battle site in France where so many Ulster soldiers lost their lives during the Battle of the Somme. This card depicts the dedication of the Ulster Division War Memorial at Theipval in November 1921. Clergy officiating at the service were Most Rev. Dr d'Arcy, Lord Primate of All Ireland, Right Rev. Dr Lowe, Moderator of the General Assembly, Rev. W.H. Smith, President of the Methodist Church in Ireland, and Rev. Dr Simms CB, CMG. General Weygard, Chief of Staff to Marshal Foch, unveiled the tablet. Lord Carson and Sir James Craig, the first Prime Minister of Northern Ireland, were unable to attend.